House Bird

Also by Robert Fillman

November Weather Spell (chapbook)

Summer Ending

—after Edward Hopper's Summer Evening

Under a dull orb of porch light, they stand
motionless. The moon rises like a skull,
and they're desperate for sound, a twig snap
or small leaf rustling, anything. He thought
he'd won her, balanced his job all summer,
fishing on the lake, kept her simmering
like a boiling pan. She leans on the wall,
her pink halter top concealing little,
her legs, long and smooth like the white clapboard.
In his dark blue shirtsleeves, hand on his heart,
he wouldn't dare drape the other across
her bare upper arm, at least not tonight.
But he would love to slip fingers through her
hair. He imagined the way he'd trail them,
as if a slack hand rippling the water's
shimmery surface. She'd take off her top
and skirt, beckon him into the night air.
He'd undress, follow. But their eyes never
meet. She's lost, turning away, seeming to
look beyond the soles of her tennis shoes,
into the future, into the dry grain
of her stiffened heart. The closed door, a small
gap in the curtains, people in the house
probably sleeping, inches between them,
summer is ending on her parents' porch.
But they are silent, unable to move,
afraid to take even a single breath.

Five

Hunting Season

The day after Thanksgiving,
        our stomachs
not yet settled from all the turkey
        and ham,
we got out our coloring books.
Dad started packing his gear,
        an old sleeping bag,
        blaze orange hunting jacket,
        blankets and beer,
Mom stood in the kitchen
        slicing
onion and turkey for sandwiches.
We listened to her crinkling
wax paper into perfect folds
as she neatly tucked in the ends
before filling his thermos with coffee
        for the long
drive north. My brothers and I sat
on the couch, the blue light
        of the TV
        flashing
raw resentment. That's when Dad
tiptoed into the parlor, kissed
        our foreheads
        and disappeared.
What he said if anything
we didn't hear. Our bodies barely shifting,
like logs in a fire that had already
        gone cold.

The Batter

One pitch a little too high
and inside, Bobby Smiegel,
who had been on the losing

end of it, both on the field
and at home, mulling the sting
of that rubber ball, so much

like his father's belt smacking
the backs of his thighs, how he
couldn't duck out of the way,

how boys laughed at his squeals
as he writhed on the ground in pain,
it took no more than seconds

for him to snap, all of that
hurt from Bobby's heart channeled
into that bat, exploding

with a single swat against
a tree, which could have been one
of us on his knees begging

for his life, the others all
watching in horror what might
have been, as rumor has it,

House Bird

Robert Fillman

Terrapin Books

Terrapin Books
4 Midvale Avenue
West Caldwell, NJ 07006

www.terrapinbooks.com

ISBN: 978-1-947896-52-9
Library of Congress Control Number: 2021951375

First Edition

Cover art by Jason Martin

Contents

For Melissa, Emma, and Robert
and in memory of my grandfather, Robert Feller

Cleaning out the basement closet

beneath the stairs, I come across
a deck of dirty playing cards
from a friend's bachelor party

and holding fifty-two women
in my hand I suddenly think
of my grandfather's coal cellar

in the back corner of his house,
how dark it seemed, the way the light
only shafted in from its one

narrow window, how at thirteen
I spent hours helping my pap crush
bags of aluminum cans we'd

later haul to the scrap yard, sell
for a few measly bucks, but I
also recall the portrait that

hung on the interior door,
a beautiful woman, half-nude,
hidden from my grandmother's view,

painted mostly in blues, except
for the red of her lips, the white
of her pastel breasts, the raw pink

of her nipples, like bull's-eyes on
a chest that seemed to lean forward
whenever my grandfather's back

was turned, as if asking to be
kissed if he happened to leave the room.

One

A Creation Story

I can still remember
the splintered black pieces

of my brother's only
video game cartridge

exploding from beneath
the heel of Dad's work boot

after an argument.
Like the Big Bang, shards spread

across the shiny white
tile of the kitchen floor,

scattering a private
matter throughout the old

neighborhood and beyond.
In those milliseconds

after the initial shock,
our jaws unlatched as our

hearts sped into a space
that allowed for only

one center. Our fresh tears
magnified our father—

the cold, bright force
we feared and loved.

The Frame Maker's Hands

No one would question him,
would challenge the markings
on the frame maker's hands,
veins like flashes of fox
along a field's ditch bank,
but speak across fences
and string barbed wire rumors,
stories about the girl
with the child running down
the backstairs. Recreant,
they would whisper and chase
themselves away from truth
the way a mouse flinches
just before it springs a trap,
their tongues gone chalky, fat
and slow, too much rolling
behind the upper teeth.
Later, they'd taste the soil
of root vegetables fresh
from the garden outside
his workshop in the barn,
not wanting anything
to happen, withdrawing
a little, still neighbors,
his soft hands sometimes scuffed
from sharp edges they guessed.

Woman at the Automat

—*after Edward Hopper's* Automat

Looking down at her late night
coffee cup, she sits alone,
back to the window, her legs

close together but exposed
beneath the slick, round table,
a wood chair across from her.

Her red lips hover above
pale breasts, but that yellow hat
like a soft moan obscures her eyes,
makes you wonder what she wants,
if it would take a lifetime.

She served herself tonight, dropped
a few nickels in the slot,
took her meal at the table
near the never-closing door
by the radiator's warmth,
the bowl of red plastic fruit

in the window to her rear.
How the night might close inward,
but those legs shining bright,
she sits openly for me.

Rattails

All the neighborhood boys had them.
Ricky Conrad was first, and then
Devon Feldman and Jayden Wartz.

Bobby Smiegel got his too late
in the year, always untucking
his blond wisps from those turtlenecks

his mother dressed him in for school.
Dev sported his like the mud flaps
drooping from his dad's battered Dodge.

Jayden's seemed to drift on the wind,
soft curls trailing him like rings of
cigarette smoke. Ricky lost his

before us all. We found him crouched
barefoot beneath his uncle's porch,
blood dried on his lip, two black eyes

forming a single drainage ditch.
He held out a hand, the last strands
of his childhood trapped in his palm.

Cicadas

All week cicadas have rattled
above me as I walk behind
the lawn mower, or when
I'm crouched collecting baseballs
the neighbor's kids accidentally
chucked into our yard, or standing
naked, dripping in the shower.
Here it is, the last week in July,
summer beginning to come to a close.
A chorus curls up from within
the tree line, rising and getting
sharper, a yellow fluttering
sound, like a fog crusting over
and settling, seeping into cracked
window seals, the slats of lawn chairs,
burrowing its way into walls.
The days have been getting shorter
for a month. It's as if we've been
scared to speak of fireflies sparking
in the backyard after supper,
or the way the Fourth sidled up
and disappeared like smoke after
dousing the coals. How the season
pulses gently and then circles
louder, louder, reaching us all,
then quiets, littering ashes—
dried-out brown shells, forked, tiny claws
hooked on branches well into fall.
And we, listening even then,
trying to remember those calls.

Crows Siren

Their calls echo

off gray bark,
rusted wrought iron,

low hanging
clouds. They sober

the yawn of
an afternoon,

murder red
orange leaves, burning

them before
they fall scattered

against the still
lush green lawn.

Driving to the Jeweler's Shop

My wife wants me to get
my wedding band resized
because it hasn't fit
since I lost weight. I stopped
wearing it months ago,
afraid I'd lose it, that
it would fly off again,
find its way down a drain
or sewer grate, maybe
disappear in the lawn
among the rotting green
shells of the black walnut
that litter our backyard,
the weight of its absence
felt most when I bring her
hand into mine, lift it
to my lips, feel her cold
metal against my skin,
which sends her slight request
whirling into the air,
weightless and heavy all
at once, just like our vows,
which are as snug today
as the day we spoke them,
easier to honor
than they are to forget.

Service Record

Your oil burner was inspected and maintained
on *12/21/19 64* by *Vince*,
the tag said.

It was mild that day, 51 degrees,
good visibility, no rainfall,
warm for December. By Christmas
it was cold again, not bitter—
I checked the *Farmer's Almanac*.

I wonder if you celebrated Christmas,
if your family counted on you,
especially that time of year.
What did you carry in your lunch pail?
Was that thermos filled with coffee?

For some reason, I picture you
mid-fifties, browline glasses,
frosted hair combed back, maybe
a gray workmen's jacket
over your coveralls, your name
sewn on the left breast pocket—*Vince*.
I imagine you worked for that oil company
your whole adult life,
loyal, dependable, respected, always
one to show a new guy the ropes.
I bet when you passed
your neighbor on your walk to work,
you stopped, greeted him with a smile.

(Of course, you walked to work.
That's just the type of thing you did.)

When my wife and I bought this house
three years ago, the previous owners
took us on a tour.
They had lived here since 1946,
so I'm sure they met you, Vince.
I remember how they walked us
into the basement, to the furnace—
a monstrosity,

a brown behemoth, warm to the touch,
rattling and chugging away, spewing
hot air like the boilers in *Titanic*.
The entire place reeked of oil.

We replaced the thing
once we moved in—
after it was condemned.
The service man, whose name
I cannot remember,
called it a fire hazard,
so we put in a highboy,
efficient, sleek, new.

While cleaning out the basement
yesterday, I came across a yellow tag
which I am certain had been
secured to the furnace by your hand,
had some years later fallen off,
and had rested

on the cold, damp concrete,
unnoticed ever since.

I picked it up and read:
Your furnace was inspected and maintained
on *12/21/19 64* by *Vince*.
Thank you for your patronage! Hope to see you next year!
Your scrawl, our only correspondence.

The Night John Lennon Was Killed

In the small middle bedroom of our two-story row home,
I sat on the floor, legs crossed, my mom's old Beatles albums

scattered all around, John's warm baritone flowing into
my young ears, imparting lessons about the human heart.

Not even in grade school, and yet I had already learned
the language of LPs and 45s, with their swirling

orange and yellow labels, the bright Capitol rainbow.
Mom bought blank cassettes, showed me how to press "record" if one

of our favorites came on the radio. She tuned me
to the music of our blood, showed me the photos of her

as a child slinging her hips to the same rock 'n' roll songs
I loved, one arm held above her head, steadied by the grip

of my grandfather, a life before I arrived. As long
as that needle pressed on those records, John's words wrapped around

me and kept me safe, as though cradled in my mother's arms.
That all ended one day when I asked her if The Beatles

still made music. My mom told me, *No, John Lennon is dead*.
A revolving black circle of quiet followed, spinning

around me at first and then spreading beyond the bedroom,
seeming to fill every dark corner of the house. That death

was like a scratch on vinyl, the turntable of my mind
tripping over tragedy, unable to get past it.

Even now, ears still ringing, I want to turn it over,
see what truth it is b/w, but the song never changes.

The record keeps repeating, *tell me why, tell me why, tell
me why, tell me why, tell me why, tell me why, tell me why—*

Two

I sit in the passenger seat

my head stuffed in a plastic bag,
replaying the terrible sins
I'd committed to deserve
this fate, insisting to myself
no more longneck bottles after
pills, no more reaching out a hand
to twirl the wisps of Jenny's hair
in geometry class, no more
forged detention slips and sneaking
out late, my dad hitting sixty
at every straight away, jerking
to a stop, speeding up again,
the windows rolled all the way down
in the five-below, and I am
repeating *Oh God* between heaves,
I'm sorry under every breath,
him driving me home, pretending
not to hear, saying nothing, once
adjusting the mirror before
he placed a cold palm on my neck
as if granting absolution.

House Bird

—after Andrew Wyeth's Bird in the House

The evening light dislodged it
from its perch, shot it straight through

an open window, stone-gray
stopped on the mantel. How quiet

the bird became. It might be
straining silver, or pulling

the summer's edge from its beak,
which tastes of goldenrod

and zinnia seeds and mud.
Hardly anyone can tell

if it's confused or afraid.
It has settled in the light

of the sun the way you'd listen
politely to your best friend

who's promised to read your palm,
a heartbeat of disbelief

rattling against dumb luck.
Shadows cringe in its presence.

The potted fern disappears.
It's the leaning bird we want

to apprehend. It doesn't
seem convinced it's not alive.

Commercial for a Midlife Crisis

The vanishing glow
of December sunset
through a bay window

betrays a daughter,
her wet moon smile,

breast bones exposed
like sweating basement pipes

no longer concealed
by sheer rose-print.

She slides backward, feels
the shriveled yank
of an incision,

embarrassment
at the thought

of her own mother,
eyebrows like cleavers,

changing
brown, bloody gauze,

over and over
the way she reassured

men would still love her
like so many
paper hearts.

Pulling off the Outlet Covers

Last night I walked around the house
pulling off the outlet covers
in every room, the small plastic

circles of protection that we
depended on those early years.
Slipping the butter knife behind,

prying them loose from their sockets
and tossing them in a bag, I
suddenly tasted the flared chill

of gin on my tongue summer nights
we danced down our layers, cast shame
into the hamper by the bed—

where you sometimes flung the condom
wrapper in the dark by mistake.
We could be so quiet, always

listening for the floors to creak,
an electric shuffle of feet
surging down the hall to our door.

Blessing

Leaving the old place for the last
time. Got the trash out, a couple
boxes in the car, the final

walk-through over. It's amazing
to see the place empty. I hope
the new owners will find as much

happiness as we did. As I'm
about to lock away the years,
abandon the memories of

dancing in the dark and my wife's
full pregnant belly warm against
my ear while I listen for our

daughter's first thoughts, I wonder if
the energy we leave behind
from living well is a blessing.

Just in case I rub hands across
plaster, squeeze every brass doorknob,
make my way outside, where I raise

my arms beneath the full moon, cast
a spell at the point of the roof
aiming to protect every brick,
every shingle of crumbling slate.

Salting the Driveway (with Help)

Salting the driveway and suddenly
I'm wrestling with questions: will my wife
and kids get home safely from shopping?

Who's watching me fling handfuls of salt
on the asphalt? Is this all there is?
I lift my head to the sky, see flakes

falling fast, nearly lose my balance
as the weight of it all covers me,
thinking this snow is no different

than the snow that fell years ago on
my grandfather, that he's probably
seen every mistake I've made. He squats

beside me, points to a patch of black
ice I've missed, says the temperature
will dip over night, that the trees will

all be shackled with ice, just wait till
morning when the sun shines on them.
He scolds me for not stepping out sooner.

Then he sighs, tells me it's okay, looks
like he wants to say more, but a wind
slips down my neck, an icy wetness

that makes me shiver almost as much
as the thought of him gone, which he is
once more, lost in the black air, so I

button up for warmth and listen for
my wife's tires lisp over slush, knowing
I will sigh too when I finally

see her headlights pull into the drive,
help them out of the car, walk each one
by the hand up the steps and into

the house and then carefully follow
after, the grocery bags over-
spilling my arms. I imagine them

smiling at me as though I were that
same man they had left an hour before.
And how would they know any different?

Talking Over a Classic Rock FM Station

The empties lie on the lawn
like a thousand cuts, bright red
cans of Coke for me, dull red

Old Milwaukee cans for him,
my uncle's crumpled heart tossed,
spread among the uncut grass,

its drunken owner cast out
of his house again, angry
at something, though I'm not sure

what, unpaid bills, the younger
daughter he caught smoking pot,
the older one that ran off

last year, barely seventeen,
pregnant with her first, my aunt
tired of his temper, telling

him not to come back this time.
It will be okay, I want
to say, but those words don't come

and he's not talking. Instead
he listens to me go on
about school, about the books

I've read, about that cute blond
from seventh period, how
we're no longer dating, how

I must have said something wrong,
about how his initials
are the same as mine. I keep

on talking, talking, talking
while his truck radio plays
one song after another

until one of us gets up
the nerve to set down his drink,
walk across the yard, shut it off—

Elegy for My Cousin Laura

My ear still warm with the news,
I walk past your house and think
about all those nights we sat
on the cold linoleum
in the kitchen, fingertips
guiding the heart-shaped plastic
across your mom's Ouija board.
We tried to summon spirits
in the dark, a dim candle-
lit circle the only way
I saw the fear in your eyes,
your trembling body trying
to hold steady as letters
came slowly, one at a time.
Certainly this was child's play,
words soaring into the air
that turned out to mean nothing,
yet as children we believed
that we could cross into that
forbidden realm where the dead
listen for their names, failing
to realize then that one day
we'd be on the other side.

Three

Hide and Seek

While tea boiled in the kettle,
my grandmother's head circled
for the culprit who'd claimed her
whistle. No bedroom corner
was safe to hide it in. She always
found it no matter how much
distance we put between her
and us. Hands of the big clock
in the hall ticking away,
a squeak from her old sneakers,
we heard every closet door
she opened and closed, the swoosh
of her housecoat, her sweet voice
asking from the stairs if we
wanted a peppermint stick,
another bottle of Coke.
She tried to lure us with love
but we knew better, as we
waited for the wool blanket
we had tossed over ourselves
to be thrown in the air, that
screech of triumph searing our
ears—the trophy always snug
in her lips before the tea
bubbled and burned on the stove.

He Plants Seeds

Down at the end of the lot,
kneeling in the loam, two hands
held out like a heart, this spring

he opens himself slowly
and pours a handful of seed
into the hole, listening

for a moment to each sing
of salvation, such language
vanishing into the trees

above him, like the dashes
and dots of Morse code he learned
in the service. Now he reads

the light that the sun scatters,
the grubs and worms he unearths
as he probes his trowel, hidden

water like a secret held
delicately in his mind.
After he covers the pile,

but before he can move down
the row, he winnows a bit
of dirt through darkened fingers

as his father had taught him,
taking a moment to breathe
the scent lodged beneath his nails.

All day long there'd been papers

—*after Harry Humes'* "Reading Late by a Simple Light"

All day long there'd been papers
to grade, students with questions,
travel expenses to file,
faculty meetings. And yet
late in the day, he slipped out
his windowless cinderblock
office hole, tiptoed away
from fluorescent bulbs, the framed
motel art posters. He crept
across campus alone, stopped

at a nearby field, listened
for a crow, the dry crumple
of leaves. A stray vee of geese
winged overhead and out of
view. He sat by a stream,
thought about Thanksgiving break
as he let the scent of earth
breathe its dim life of decay
into his bones. After that

he turned back, taking each step
a bit slower than the one
before, beginning to hum,
his voice like a radio
almost caught between stations.
He told himself to hold on

to this feeling, the fall term
not quite done. He'd have it then—
for collecting his teaching
things, on the long drive home, when
there was nothing but static.

The Art of Writhing

Never turn over
a bucket to
find a poem coiled,

waiting,
inviting you
to pick it up.

It slithers away,
crawling to some
dark spot between rocks,

macadam roads at night
trying to soak
up the remaining

heat that radiates in
things, or probing
its muscular body

along the thin wire fence
of a backyard,
where tall weeds

shield it from screeching
hawks or large hands
wielding a shovel.

Only the fastest dares
pounce, gets up nerve
to strike, sinks fangs deep,

risks poisoning itself
to bring life to
that once flicking tongue.

The Optimist

My wife's fuzzy socks might
have freckles. Some are pink
or gray from heel to toe.
Others are striped. When she
peels them off her sweating
feet and tosses them on
the floor beside the bed
in the middle of night,
I am always asleep.
But every morning
while I'm making the bed,
I find them lying there
together, and I smile.
I hear her downstairs
laughing with the children,
and I pick up the pair,
twirl it limp in my hand,
then rub my thumb across
a ribbed elastic cuff
before dropping them in
the hamper. I never
know if I'm supposed to.
They always smell so fresh.

The Second Offer

When I want to thaw out
my regrets I can drive
to the house we almost
bought together, exit
the car and descend that
steep hill of memory—
not the flowerless yard,
all rocks and dried weeds, stiff
against the gray shingles
and harsh glare of winter.
Instead, I contemplate
you circling the shade tree
we discovered out back
that April afternoon,
FOR SALE sign no longer
hammered into the lawn,
your hands darkened by dirt,
the prayer you whispered
among the heart-shaped leaves
and first sprouts of blood root
yarrow and chicory,
overgrown with desire,
what you'd do to the place—
contrite that I never
made a second offer.

The Card Trick

Don't tell, he whispered in my ear,
making me promise never to
say a word to my kid brother,
or the bully at school who clenched
my balls in his fist as a joke
on the playground, making me writhe
on the numbered chalk in front of
Maggie Sims, our next door neighbor,
the girl I loved. He pulled me by
the neck with his cold hands, *Don't tell*,
he whispered again, *Now try it
once yourself*, handing me the deck,
the beer drifting from his breath like
a spell enchanting every king
and queen as I laid the cards on
the table in columns. He knocked
the oak with approval each time
I hit it right, collected rows
in the pattern that he taught me,
deliberate, counting backwards
slowly in my head. His eyes gleamed
under the single kitchen light
when I said he could cut the cards
as many times as he liked.
He clapped for the showmanship, that
almost-imperceptible grip

of hesitation before I
asked the master: *Is this your card?*
holding it in front of his face,
like a winning lottery stub,
half-believing the magic trapped
between a finger and a thumb.

When Kurt Cobain killed himself

I was twelve. I remember
my mother cracking open
the door to my room, scooching

beside me in bed, and then
placing her hand on the back
of my head, as if that would

somehow soften the blow or
unlodge the fragments of truth
that would surely tear apart

my pre-teen mind. And how long
really did I sit stonefaced
staring at a wall? How could

a boy's rock 'n' roll hero
die before his mom even
tells him what is for supper?

What I hadn't thought about
till I became a parent
was how hard it must have been

for my mom to share this news
with her son, a sheltered child
who had never even been

to a funeral, or helped
his dad bury a dead pet.
Now I think about how she

must have wordlessly endured
those bewildering seconds
of my school day, all the while

seeing my childhood thrashing
for its life in the seconds
before she finally slipped

that long needle of knowledge
into my flesh, having to
trust I'd come through it okay.

Lion Dream

—after Hemingway

When you dream about lions
make sure they are on a beach,
and that you're a safe distance
away. Two lions would do.
Make them young brothers romping
on the white sand, playfully
pawing at each other's maws.
One well-warmed lion twisting
on its back, while the other
lolls out its tongue to lap fur
before lounging in the sun.
An African beach is best,
some mountain's great brown body
giving back the inland breeze
as in a contest between
the breakers and the blue sky.
Make the coastline long so it
stretches into another
dream, so that when the morning
light hits your face you must tilt
your head and turn away from
the sand so bright that it burns
your eyes and makes you lose sight
of the lions on the beach
that are in your bedroom now
nuzzling your knuckles that drape
over the side of your bed.

Four

Starling in the Furnace Room

First a small, muffled twittering,
wings flapping against louvered doors,
then a strange, panicked crying sound.

My father suspecting a bat
slowly pries open the panels
while my brothers and I hold our
breath on the basement steps, asking

how the thing got in. Did it fold
itself through a crack between beams?
Did it fall through the chimney cap?

My father's hands, deft as they are,
can't defy the laws of motion.

I remember feathers flying,
a tiny heart that ceased to beat,
the afternoon suddenly dark,
trapped in iridescent silence.

Omen

The mountain as severe
as my grandfather's brow
in that small airless room
during his final hours,
I see a barn owl soar
out of the ridge's mouth,
its big head, terrible
eyes cursing all color,
as if it were hell-bent
on draining the season

of red maple, black gum—
every leaf a target.
It doesn't seem to know
the difference between
misery and mercy,
the living and the dead,
that my grandfather warned
Go easy on your kids
before he closed his eyes
and slipped away his hand.

My body suddenly
tight, bracing for a blow,
as if I am the prey,
a small, soft animal,
yet I'm surprised to feel
a fluff of brown feathers
then a rush of wings that

beats on, flooding my ears
with what could only be
the sound of a last breath.

Doo Wop Dream

All those Doo Wops have disappeared,
those 1950s Vegas-style

two-story beach rentals with their
neon signs and plastic trees, their

cookie-cutter rooms and spiral
stairways, their colorful paint jobs

and names to match: the Blue Marlin,
the Golden Sunset, the White Star.

On one of those rare occasions
when we could manage a daytrip

to the Jersey shore, my parents
and I would walk the main drag, awed

by their nostalgic charm, my mom
jotting down telephone numbers,

my dad and I wanting to peek
at the pools, see that clean swirling

water reflect the midday sun.
We never stayed at one, and they

didn't stay either, replaced by
apartments, condominiums,

the same space but none of the pop.
Older now, I see how tacky

those U and L-shaped motels were,
that what they offered was not quite

real, a glimpse into another
kind of life, one I'd never know.

What really would have happened had
we squeezed into one of those rooms,

my parents on the pull-out, me
on the loveseat. What if we had

hung towels on the balcony,
sipped coffee from the cups we found

in our very own kitchenette,
tossed crumbs to gulls that flocked beneath

those artificial palms as we
let that salty air cure our dreams.

My Wife Returns to the Pew After Communion

She eyes me like a mural
on the church wall, a heart-shaped
whisper between two lovers

suspended for a moment,
and I can no longer hear
our kids stomping down the aisle

or feel the surging organ.
Instead I sense her warm breath
slinking beneath my collar,

the hairs on my neck wrinkling
at the thought of her body
wet and heavenly against

my chest, her perfume on my
fingers from the night before,
everyone staring at her

great ass when she bends to sit.
So I give thanks, drop a few
extra coins into the plate.

Witness

Probably by now, my friend
has recovered from the shock
of finding his pet rooster
headless and strung to the fence.
He has no doubt untangled
the thing, his bare hands perhaps
sticky with feathers and stained
with blood, the knees of his pants
maybe cool, wet from kneeling
on damp earth, having buried
the bird, taking care to smooth
the mound with a shovel, still
not realizing what transpired,
how he had hunted it down
before dawn and drunk with rage
bent over its body, choked
last crows from its throat and stole
the morning light from its eyes
before returning to his
home and probably crawling
into bed, without knowing
what he was capable of,
how late he'd sleep, what silence
would follow his every step
when he finally started
his long list of daily chores.

Promises

My father didn't talk
much to me as a kid.
So each sentence glimmered

as if it reflected
his eyes and not the mug
of beer lifted beneath

the yellow kitchen light
those nights on Union Street.
My son's hesitant *Yes*

I would like that brings me
back to words my father
never said but guided

into me with his hands,
the even syllables
of a saw pulled across

a two-by-four, the rasp
of a taping knife scraped
over spackle, the smack

of an old baseball trapped
in the web of his glove.
Each act translated back

to a promise of love,
the only way he knew
how to cure the silence.

For Snowflake

Here I am again, elbows
propped on the cold kitchen tile,
trying to scoop up the chunks
of slimy chicken, lifting

the spoon, hoping the kitten
will eat this time, at least slurp
some of the gravy that has
puddled in his bowl. It's my

son's three-month-old cat, the one
he woke to Christmas morning,
snuggled with every night since,
carried in his arms, held close

to his heart, the one the vet
warned was not growing the way
it ought, not gaining any
weight because it probably

had a liver shunt, couldn't
filter toxins from its blood.
Here I am again, my nose
inches above the stinking

meat, tears flashing in my eyes
when I think of the scraggly
gray thing dying in my arms,
the soft, ragged part of me

that will die too when I break
the news to my son, those words
prowling closer and closer,
stopping only to preen and
stare at me unblinkingly.

Superstition

Don't bathe in a thunderstorm,
my mother would say. Lightning

can strike. I think of this as
I watch from the tub, each flash,

a split second closer to
my wife tapping on the door,

jimmying the lock when she
gets no answer, finding me

dead, body still warm and soft
against the white porcelain.

But nothing ever happens.
And I do not want to go,

not yet, not while water rolls
down the curves of my shoulders

in beads, not without raising
my hands in prayer, not until

I can pull back the curtain
satisfied that I am clean.

Summer Ending

—*after Edward Hopper's* Summer Evening

Under a dull orb of porch light, they stand
motionless. The moon rises like a skull,
and they're desperate for sound, a twig snap
or small leaf rustling, anything. He thought
he'd won her, balanced his job all summer,
fishing on the lake, kept her simmering
like a boiling pan. She leans on the wall,
her pink halter top concealing little,
her legs, long and smooth like the white clapboard.
In his dark blue shirtsleeves, hand on his heart,
he wouldn't dare drape the other across
her bare upper arm, at least not tonight.
But he would love to slip fingers through her
hair. He imagined the way he'd trail them,
as if a slack hand rippling the water's
shimmery surface. She'd take off her top
and skirt, beckon him into the night air.
He'd undress, follow. But their eyes never
meet. She's lost, turning away, seeming to
look beyond the soles of her tennis shoes,
into the future, into the dry grain
of her stiffened heart. The closed door, a small
gap in the curtains, people in the house
probably sleeping, inches between them,
summer is ending on her parents' porch.
But they are silent, unable to move,
afraid to take even a single breath.

Five

Hunting Season

The day after Thanksgiving,
        our stomachs
not yet settled from all the turkey
        and ham,
we got out our coloring books.
Dad started packing his gear,
        an old sleeping bag,
          blaze orange hunting jacket,
          blankets and beer,
Mom stood in the kitchen
        slicing
onion and turkey for sandwiches.
We listened to her crinkling
wax paper into perfect folds
as she neatly tucked in the ends
before filling his thermos with coffee
        for the long
drive north. My brothers and I sat
on the couch, the blue light
        of the TV
        flashing
raw resentment. That's when Dad
tiptoed into the parlor, kissed
        our foreheads
        and disappeared.
What he said if anything
we didn't hear. Our bodies barely shifting,
like logs in a fire that had already
        gone cold.

The Batter

One pitch a little too high
and inside, Bobby Smiegel,
who had been on the losing

end of it, both on the field
and at home, mulling the sting
of that rubber ball, so much

like his father's belt smacking
the backs of his thighs, how he
couldn't duck out of the way,

how boys laughed at his squeals
as he writhed on the ground in pain,
it took no more than seconds

for him to snap, all of that
hurt from Bobby's heart channeled
into that bat, exploding

with a single swat against
a tree, which could have been one
of us on his knees begging

for his life, the others all
watching in horror what might
have been, as rumor has it,

one barrel later exchanged
for another, but back then
we couldn't have known how close
Bobby was to his final out.

Toast

My wife at work by 4 a.m.,
I'm making breakfast for the kids,
scraping big squares of cold butter
across toast, the knife's edge tearing
bread, and I think about how this
one imperfection will ruin
my daughter's morning, how she will
complain and refuse even to
take a bite, her brother waking
to her whines. Then I imagine
what I would do differently
the next time: Am I still married
at thirty-seven? Do I take
that job in Nevada? Should I
tell my family I've been drunk
more than a week, that I never
asked for buttered toast, or a cup
of instant coffee and cartoons
for my life. As I crunch the blade
across the stacked slices, burnt crumbs
stick to my hands, and I wonder
how I can disguise this mistake.

The Shell

—after Andrew Wyeth's Her Room

He left the door open
    like he always does,
the sash windows closed
    but the curtains drawn
so we can look out
    on the shore and pretend we know
where meadow brush meets
    the water. He's not forgetful.
At any moment he'll appear
    at the door, home for supper.
As a young man, he pushed us
    to argue for the sun half hidden
by the midday haze,
    the sad surge of gulls.
He'd ask us to breathe
    the pebble round air of the coast,
to suck the current into our lungs
    like water that funnels between rocks.
I can see him then, all sinew,
    pointing toward the scalloped white shell
orphaned on the desk.
    Lift it, he'd say, lean the opening
to your ear, turn it in a certain way,
    until you become a pilgrim,
yourself a rimless tunnel
    gliding toward the surf
and its cloaked gravelly bottom
    that shifts but never warns
how steep the drop-off is.

The Bones

What I remember most
are the bones—and my dad's
fingers slimy with guts

as he pulled apart bits
of smoked whiting he'd bought
from the market downtown.

He sat in the kitchen
most of the afternoon,
working over headless

glistening flesh, picking
through the soft pink insides
without a knife or fork,

offering my brother
and me a horse-radished
peck now and then. We stood

by his side and waited,
listened to him humming
along with Merle Haggard

between long sips of beer.
He was always careful
with the giving, his hands

like a slow, warm current
feeding another. That
cold fish with its many

bones. Dad never let one
slip past. It was all smoke
and silver scales, the tang
of root wet in our mouths.

Schuylkill County Ghost Story, 1932

Neither boy knew what to do.
No rabbit where their father
had pointed, only gravestones.

They dared not question his aim,
or his decision to fire
into a moonlit churchyard.

A scarce meal but meal enough
for the family of three,
worth risking a shot at dusk
with winter frost on their heels.

They only wondered where it
went. Dad never missed. Could it
have skipped the wall? They saw no
trail of blood. No sign at all.

But then they heard a crackling
in the bushes, something to
draw eyes from the spot they'd been
staring at. When they turned back,

the evening suddenly pale,
their faces a sickly gray,

they saw the shadow of what
had once been a man tossing
dinner over his shoulder.

The Garden

She's out again at the lawn's edge
in her shorts, hose with the special
plant food attachment, gardening
gloves soaked, water having run down
the soft white curves of her forearm.
In the grass by her feet, a pile
of tangled roots and damaged stems.
She has planted the mums beside
her favorite hydrangea
in these still-warm days of autumn.
Almost kneeling, she takes a bloom
into her palm, inches closer,
her lips touching the pink blossom
the way I sometimes kiss her
bare shoulder. Watching from the porch,
I see her calves tense as she steps
back like a satisfied artist.
I want to call out to her,
or gently approach as she works.
But she squeezes the nozzle then,
and I am sent away wishing
I deserved the snugness of that touch.

The Snake Man's Lesson

My neighbor Sid collected snakes,
had a basement filled with them, each
held in a house of glass. Sid walked

us down to watch him feed baby
mice to his saddle-brown boa.
He dangled a white creature by

its tail above the tank so we
could see its tiny pink eyes and
tiny pink ears twitching as it

struggled and thrashed to stay alive.
Sid's grip was firm in hand and mind.
His smile made us squirm, shield faces.

He promised it was over,
got us to uncover our eyes
in time to see that muscular

shiny body coiling around
its motionless prey. Years later,
I learned he was a professor

of wildlife management, who taught
us that death meant life, shed light on
the other side of the story
and dared us to look—

The Blue Hour

Twenty years since I stood waiting
by the third-floor bedroom window
at dusk, thinking about the ghost
stories my grandfather recycled
those cold Pennsylvania days
just after we set back the clocks,
gained the extra blue hour of light,
that sacred time when the living
and the dead can see each other.

I remember the steam whirling
from chimneys like hundreds of souls
lured by stars, stretching their new wings
beneath the moon's hollow shiver,
one chance to cross over from this
realm and sail into the flute song
of silver light—caught between worlds
for less than a second, then gone.

Twenty years since I swore I saw
Katie Estan's older sister,
fourteen, dead of meningitis,
drift past my snow-shackled rooftop,
heard her song on the wind, a voice
no longer torn by fever but pink
and sequined like the gown she wore
to the eighth grade formal just one
month before. Twenty years since she
smoldered past a wobbling Venus,
dancing her way into the dark.

Acknowledgments

My thanks to the editors of the following journals in which some of these poems, or earlier versions of them, first appeared:

About Place Journal: "Cicadas"'

Blueline: "The Shell"

Broad River Review: "The Second Offer"

The Chaffin Journal: "Service Record"

Chiron Review: "The Garden"

Cider Press Review: "Lion Dream"

Common Ground Review: "Crows Siren"

Crack the Spine: "Commercial for a Midlife Crisis"

Flint Hills Review: "The Frame Maker's Hands"

Glassworks: "Woman at the Automat"

Hamilton Stone Review: "Omen," "Promises"

The Hollins Critic: "House Bird"

I-70 Review: "Hide and Seek"

Innisfree: "Hunting Season," "Summer Ending"

Lily Poetry Review: "The Card Trick"

Main Street Rag: "My Wife Returns to the Pew After Communion," "Pulling off the Outlet Covers"

The Night Heron Barks: "The Batter"

Ninth Letter: "The Blue Hour"

North Dakota Quarterly: "Salting the Driveway (with Help)"

Off the Coast: "The Optimist"

Paterson Literary Review: "Doo Wop Dream," "Driving to the Jewelers Shop," "For Snowflake"

Pembroke Magazine: "The Art of Writhing," "Elegy for my Cousin Laura," "Talking Over a Classic Rock FM Station"

Poet Lore: "A Creation Story," "Toast"

Poetry East: "Rattails"

Slipstream: "The Night John Lennon Was Killed," "When Kurt Cobain killed himself"

Split Rock Review: "Witness"

Sugar House Review: "I sit in the passenger seat"

Tar River Poetry: "The Bones," "Cleaning Out the Basement Closet," "Superstition"

Third Wednesday: "Blessing," "The Snake Man's Lesson"

Valparaiso Poetry Review: "He Plants Seeds"

The Westchester Review: "Starling in the Furnace Room"

"All day long there'd been papers" was published in *Keystone: Contemporary Poets on Pennsylvania*, eds. Marjorie Maddox and Jerry Wemple (Penn State University Press, 2025).

"Superstition" was reprinted in *The Strategic Poet*, ed. Diane Lockward (Terrapin Books, 2021).

"The Blue Hour," "A Creation Story," "House Bird," "Rattails," "Service Record," and "Superstition" appeared in *November Weather Spell* (Main Street Rag, 2019).

My special thanks to Eric Chiles and Bob Watts for their insightful comments about many of the poems in this book. As always, my deepest gratitude to my family for their encouragement, continual support, and, most of all, love.

About the Author

Robert Fillman is the author of the chapbook *November Weather Spell* (Main Street Rag, 2019). His poems have appeared in such journals as *The Hollins Critic*, *Poetry East*, *Salamander*, *Spoon River Poetry Review*, and *Tar River Poetry*. His criticism has been published by *ISLE: Interdisciplinary Studies in Literature and the Environment*, *CLAJ: The College Language Association Journal*, and elsewhere. He holds a Ph.D. in English from Lehigh University, teaches at Kutztown University, and lives in Macungie, Pennsylvania, with his wife and their two children. Earlier versions of this collection were named finalist for both the Cider Press Review Book Award and the Gerald Cable Book Award. This is Fillman's debut full-length collection.

www.robertfillman.com